STEAMO
GOES TO HAVANA

By Michael Miller

Illustrations by Jeffrey Vernon

NEW FALCON PUBLICATIONS

Copyright © 2022 Michael Miller

All rights reserved. No part of this book, in part or in whole, may be reproduced, transmitted, or utilized, in any form or by any means, electronic or mechanical, including photocopying, recording, or by any information storage and retrieval system, without permission in writing from the publisher, except for brief quotations in critical articles, books and reviews.

ISBN 13: 978-1-56184-505-7
ISBN 10: 1-56184-505-1

First Edition 2022

The paper used in this publication meets the minimum requirements of the American National Standard for Permanence of Paper for Printed Library Materials Z39.48-1984

Printed in USA

NEW FALCON PUBLICATIONS
2046 Hillhurst Avenue
Los Angeles, CA 90027

info@newfalcon.com
newfalcon.com

Acknowledgements

The author wants to happily acknowledge and greedily thank the following awesome people without whom this unusual book would have likely remained just an interesting idea:

Minhee Choe, Jeff Vernon,
Dr. Liz, Ed Dornberger, Chuck Parcell,
Bruce Herman, Johnny Cochran,
and Egor Shpak.

All these wonderful people played different and important roles in motivating and expanding on ideas for the author. Without this motivation and these ideas Steamo wouldn't be the amazing wonder crab he turned out to be.

A profound and heartfelt thank you is expressed to all the readers of this book.

Steamo in Havana

Steamo's Pillars of Life Success

1. You can be right or be happy and you can't be both - so choose wisely.
2. When life gives you Lemons make lemonade. Always Turn a negative into two positives, find a way.
3. Anything worth having is worth working for, so work for it if you want it.
4. The process is more important than the outcome - enjoy the ride.
5. Although it's extremely hard to do Be honest with yourself - a half truth is the same thing as a lie so be extremely mindful not to deceive yourself.
6. A beginning is more than half of the whole. So just start.
7. Forget being lucky. The harder you work the luckier you get.
8. Ego is the enemy. Stay humble.
9. Action makes words unnecessary. Be a person who takes action, and always under-promise and over deliver.
10. Be impeccable with your word always and in all ways.
11. Know the difference between hearing and listening and act accordingly.
12. Do what's best for you - always and in all ways. In the end that's what's best for the people around you too.
13. Control the controllables.
14. Don't give up: "I will persist until I succeed."
15. Don't get distracted by The Who Who Ha Ha, that's the most expensive item on earth.

Introduction

The Indigenous People of Cuba and Other Remote Caribbean Islands

It's an extremely tragic tale. Starting with day one of Columbus arriving, there was massive enslavement of the natives and physical assaults including rape against small children.

Columbus recorded in his journal how wonderful it was that he and his men could have sex with children even though it was forbidden in Spain.

Consider the story of Alexander the Great. His father was Philip of Macedonia. When Philip was a child Macedonia was a vassal state to Athens (subjugated tributary state) and in this capacity he was taken to Athens as a treaty hostage. This was an institution that really doesn't exist in the modern world but was very common in the ancient world.

As a prepubescent, Phillip was given as a catamite (a sex slave) to the Praetorian Guard (palace guard - an elite combat unit). In the fullness of time Philip grew to manhood and was returned to his homeland. Then the Peloponnesian war happened.

Athens and Sparta fought the Peloponnesian war and both sides were exhausted at the end leaving a power vacuum on the Greek mainland.

Philip grew to power in Macedonia during this power vacuum and conquered the Greek mainland including Athens.

And his very first act when he came to power was to execute every single member of the Praetorian Guard.

As an aside Churchill once said British Navy tradition consists of rum, the lash and sodomy. The tradition of the cabin boy says it all. Months at sea and no women; one plus one equals two.

Going back to Columbus; freed from the normal moral and legal bounds of Europe and Spain he and his men just went wild and they did whatever they wanted with the natives in Cuba. He shamelessly recorded this in his journal including the detailed descriptions of the tortures they inflicted upon the natives. Things like burning them alive and cutting their hands and feet off as well as disemboweling them.

In 1506 the natives on the island of Hispaniola which is now Haiti and the Dominican Republic got together and decided to revolt.

Because they didn't have cell phones and newspapers they sent messages around from one area to another telling the other natives the revolt would occur on the first night of the full moon.

The full moon occurs in a single moment in time it's like the spring equinox. Depending on what time of day or night this moment happens and it occurs randomly throughout the day it can be difficult by the naked eye to tell which is specifically the night of the full moon.

For example the full moon may occur at noon in the daytime. So, for example the night before the night or the night after looks exactly the same or quite similar.

So one group of Indians went off the night before and the Spaniards were warned and they were able to put the revolt down.

Like the Tet offensive in Vietnam, if you have one people that's smaller and less well armed it's essential that they attack all the same time if they want to have success.

The Caribbean islands are small and they were sparsely populated by the Caribs Indian people. They were all killed of disease, murder and execution. For all intents and purposes the population was completely wiped out. Historians recognize it as a particularly tragic episode of colonialism.

In order to work the fertile land they brought in the slaves from Africa. Along with mixtures of Spaniards and other Europeans, which came in over the years they make up the current population of the Caribbean islands.

And the point of all this is to oppose it to the situation in Mexico. In Mexico 90% of the indigenous people were wiped out mostly through disease but the 10% that survived inter bread to some degree with the Europeans and the Spaniards.

So in Mexico for example they didn't need slaves, who were very expensive at the time, because agriculture was already firmly established there and they already had strong people to work the lands.

The population around Mexico City and in the surrounding region (which is called the street de federal) is the most European of all Regions in Mexico culture because of genetics and culture.

In the more remote areas of Mexico like the mountains or the southern jungles there are millions of people whose native language is still some Indian language such as Teppee in the south. These are people who don't start speaking Spanish until they're teenagers when they start getting out of the house.

Take the international date line as a motif and let's think about the cultural and genetic change as you move east from Europe into China and then pass into the New World which is how people got to the New World from the orient.

Now think about being in Europe and going the other way. The European colonization of North America occurred in the 1500-1700s.

What you meet is people that are as different from Europeans as possible. They are more different than us than the Chinese.

What are some of the characteristics of this difference and they are:

1. Epistemology what and how we know. For example traditional Mexican people know a lot about a little and they have a very small world which they know extremely intimately and well. Where as white Americans know a little about a lot and they have a much larger world and a much broader knowledge, but their knowledge of that world is much shallower and superficial.
2. Social loyalties. In the Indian or indigenous world ones primary loyalty is to the group they belong too. This loyalty trumps any personal loyalty or relationship. And with white American people it's the opposite.
3. One of the hallmarks of the Mexican gangs in Los Angeles for example and their people is they are incredibly united. Their gangs are their army; it's like the National Guard, they all know each other and they're all related. In the book 1491 it's about the state of affairs and what things were like in the year before Columbus came (for the Indians in the new world). As a consequence of accidents of geology, humans enter the New World through a very narrow passage the Bering strait land bridge. It's a funnel and it's only 3 miles wide when it existed. And it's way up there in the high sub arctic where there aren't many people to begin with, so the number of people that actually passed, is a relatively small number and they were all from the same group and tribe. Then they exploded in North America with its massive and abundant food supply and reproduced and populated all the way down to Tierra Del Fuego (the land of smokes in the southern tip of South America).

4. It is estimated that when Columbus arrived in 1492 in North and South America there was approximately 20 million Indians. Because they all descended from the same small group of people as previously noted they were much more genetically closely related than your typical Europeans. This means they think alike and they have the same emotions and generally they feel alike. They are much more similar which means they are much more amenable to be united and agreeing with each other and cooperating with each other and as a result 90% were wiped out.

5. A massive number of Indians were wiped out from diseases and epidemics from day one. For example Lewis and Clark spent the winter with Mandan Indians in the winter 1804-05 and 90% of them were wiped out in the smallpox epidemic of 1811 and 1812 Brought by European traders.

6. Chaokia is just across from St. Louis and it's the center of an extensive agricultural based Indian civilization. With a population of several million, they were called the mound builder peoples. European diseases were brought to the Atlantic coast in the 1500's. Individuals and groups fled the Europeans and arrived in this location, they brought with them European diseases. And by the time the Europeans arrived in the early 1700s most of the civilization had been completely wiped out 100 years prior by the European diseases.

7. It is well recognized by historians that the farther back you go in time the level of technology is lower and the greater degree of interpersonal violence there was in any given culture. For Example if you dig up medieval graveyards you find it one and six people died a violent death. Crucifixion was a normal established common means of execution and finally was banned in 321 A.D. Josephus records in his book the Jewish wars that after one particular revolt a little bit after Jesus died 800 prisoners of war or captives were crucified outside the walls of Jerusalem. And he records it because even in that time and place it was shocking that the people have gone so far in their methods of killing.

8. You might not realize it unless someone tells you but dying of thirst is one of the most agonizing and awful deaths that an animal or human can suffer.

And that is the cause of death from crucifixion. That's why it takes three days. Crucifixion is designed to prevent someone from bleeding out it's designed to keep them alive so they can feel pain as long as possible. They actually die of dehydration and thirst.

9. So warfare among the Indians and from the Indians against the Europeans as well as each other was note worthy for its savagery. Especially for the fact that prisoners were routinely tortured to death. They were often tied up and died of thirst or slowly burned and burned alive over the course of several days.

10. One out of hundreds of such incidents is when the Apaches had captured three prospectors in the 1880's at the headwaters of the Gilla river in Northern Arizona. They had tied their hands behind their back and hung them upside down so their heads were about 8 inches off the ground and built small fires which caused them to have all of the skin burned off their heads and faces and eventually they died of dehydration. The Apaches in the Comanches are especially known for thinking of very clever and horrific tortures.

11. That's why so many narratives and songs about the old west contain the line save the last bullet for yourself there is a very good reason for that. For example the Indians say General Custer shot himself which is most probably what he would've done rather than to be captured alive.

Mainland People vs. Island People

In mainland society there are large pyramids with the goal being to ruthlessly exploit those below them and shamelessly flatter those above them.

There are strict social guidelines with those at the top like the king or the general having the supreme authority.

This is the feudal system it's a system of subletting or sub renting authority.

In Islands people come from a culture that's more tribal. Every little village has its own unique pyramid. So island men are used to being the sole proprietor and not having a structure above or below them. They are not used to having authority imposed on them.

An example is found in Native culture where the person is used to acting and interacting like a king; verbally, emotionally and socially. And when white people come into contact with them they automatically want to install them at the bottom of their own social pyramids.

Monogamy is a Response to Agriculture and Diseases

Gonorrhea entered the human population around Roman times and became widespread among all the people traveling around the Roman Empire. Herpes was also prevalent at this time. There were edicts from early Roman times 10AD that you can't kiss in public because it would spread herpes. The thought was if you were kissing in public you were more likely to be strangers and to be one of many.

Syphilis entered the human population probably from sheep around 1500 A.D. Syphilis causes dramatically more damage to the human body than herpes or gonorrhea. Al Capone actually died of Syphilis.

In mainland agriculture societies the land is divided up in little squares and each man gets one piece to live on and work for his entire life. They are dividing women up the same way. So, the man and the woman stay together on that one little piece of land and this guarantees that he will be taking care of her and the children. And if you're monogamous you have a much less chance of catching a disease.

Agriculture separates us from the larger social network as everybody stays and works in their own little plot instead of gathering together in a large group and going ranging like was done in the hunter gatherer days.

Monogamy replaces the much larger social group with one person that you can count on, hopefully, and conditionally of course.

Table of Contents

Steamo's Pillers of Life Success   vii

Introduction   viii

Chapter 1   **Equality and Loyalty**   2

Chapter 2   **Courage and Ego**   11

Chapter 3   **Investing and Money**   29

Chapter 4   **Friends and Enemies**   42

Chapter 5   **Faith and Purpose**   59

Chapter 6   **Planning**   80

Chapter 7   **Self and Growth**   90

Chapter 8   **Romance**   114

Chapter 9   **Common Sense**   122

Chapter 10   **Anger and Punishment**   141

About the Author   151

Chapter 1
Equality and Loyalty

Steamo thinks that everyone has at least mild tourettes.

Steamo reminds us that whenever parting comes, it comes too soon.

Steamo found out that people see you, but they don't really know you.

Steamo can't control your loyalty but knows his comes from his heart.

Steamo knows you can't legislate equality.

Steamo reminds us not to compare our lives to others. There is no comparison between the sun and the moon. They both shine when it is their time.

Ever met a homeless person? What's the first thing you notice? They stink, because that is the natural state of man.

Steamo says don't talk to him about loyalty. "I am still holding secrets for those who are throwing dirt on my name!"

Steamo says that people tend to think I will forget the shit they said and did. But there is no expiration date for disrespect.

Steamo reminds us that death is the great equalizer.

Chapter 2
Courage and Ego

Steamo says if you really want to do something, you will find a way. If you don't you will find an excuse.

Steamo has learned that real criminals can't be cowards.

Steamo told Iraset Iraset "Live your life and forget your age!"

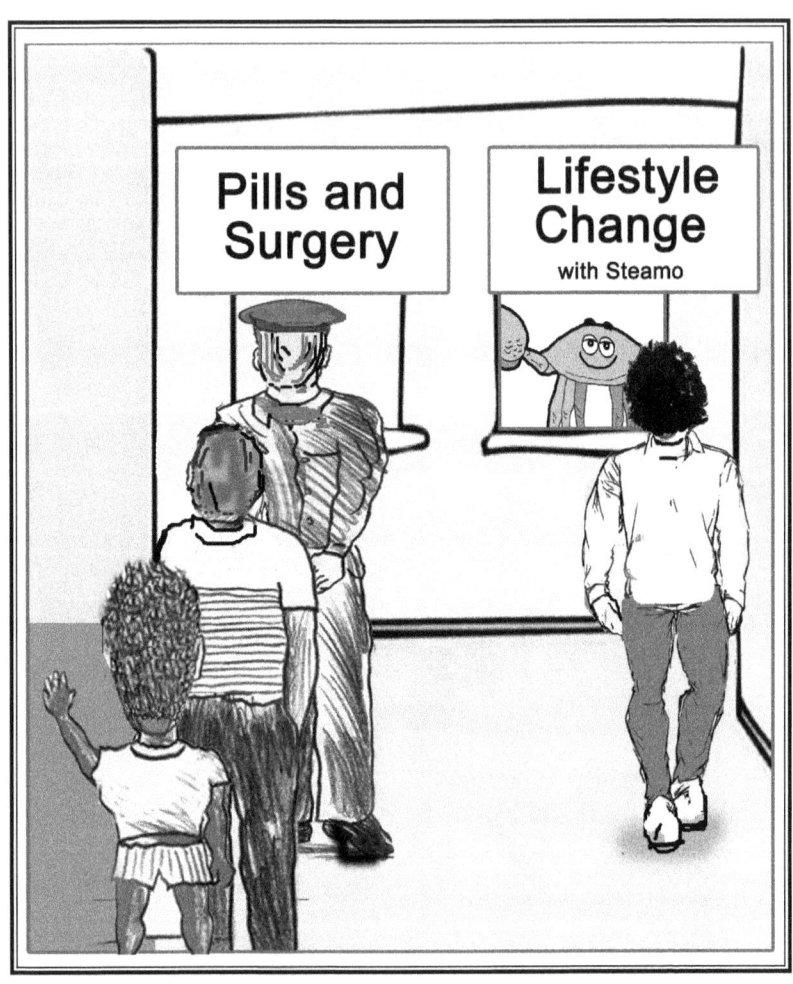

Steamo says a picture is worth a thousand words.

Steamo learned a lesson from Baseball. Both Babe Ruth and Henry Aaron struck out many times, but both hold home run records.

Steamo told Iraset Iraset that he believes an army of sheep led by a lion can defeat an army of lions led by a sheep.

Steamo says "You have to be real careful around here. You get beat up if you don't believe what everybody else believes! This is like '30's Germany!"

Steamo told his friends a dog will look down when they have done wrong. But a snake will look you right in the eye.

Steamo says the only path to real change is when there is enough pain.

Steamo knows how to build an empire with the same stones thrown at him.

Steamo says the fire inside you must be stronger than the storm outside you.

Ego is the enemy observed Steamo.

Steamo reminds us that death is not the greatest loss in life. The greatest loss is what dies inside while still alive. Never surrender!

Steamo says don't be afraid of being out-numbered. Eagles fly alone. Pigeons flock together.

Steamo says if you have been hurt many times, and you still know how to smile, trust me, you are strong!

Steamo says anyone can take a bucket of piss and call it Grandma's Peach Tea.

Steamo says "Here is a room FILLED with all the people who pay your bills, walk in your shoes every day, determine your future, and love your family way more than you possibly could."

These are the same people you should allow to discourage you. "Let that sink in."

Steamo reminds us that your mind is a magnet. If you think of blessings, you attract blessings. If you think of problems, you attract problems. Always remain optimistic!

Chapter 3
Investing and Money

Steamo says if you give a man a fish he eats for a night, but teach a man how to fish and he eats for a lifetime.

Steamo has money but it really isn't wealth. It's representative of his sacrifices, effort, relentless work and risk taking.

Steamo reminds us that rock bottom will teach you lessons that mountain tops never will.

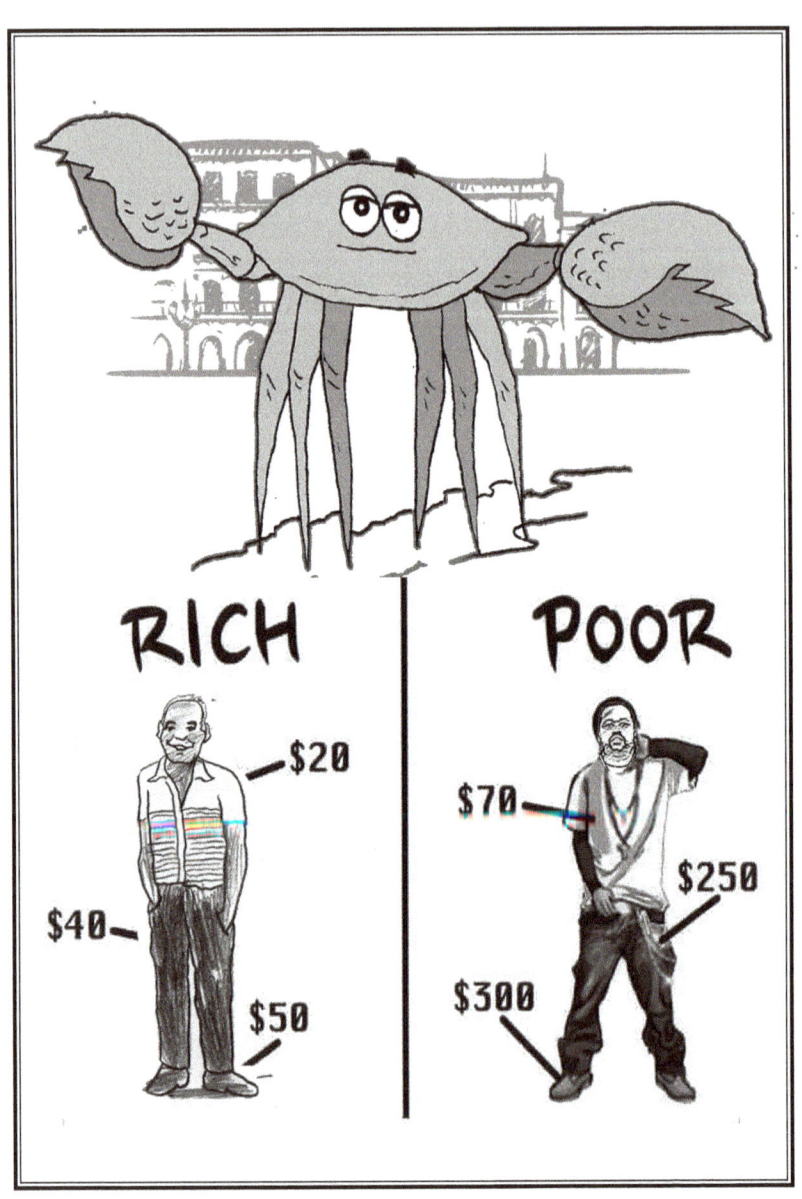

Steamo reminds us that the difference between being rich or poor can often be seen in the cartoon above.

Regarding investing, Steamo points out that pigs always get eaten.

Steamo told his rich friend Jim, if you give a person too much too soon, they will fall in love with your hand, not your heart.

Everyone has a price. One of the great struggles in life is figuring out what that price is.

Steamo says be decisive! The road of life is paved with flat squirrels who couldn't make a decision.

Steamo says parsimony can run deep in our veins!

Steamo often wonders aout equal opportunity vs. equal outcome.

Steamo says the most precious gift that you can give to someone is your time and attention.

Steamo thinks of the stock market as a giant open air casino!

Steamo reminds us that real success usually comes to those who are too busy to be looking for it!

Chapter 4
Friends and Enemies

Steamo says be careful who you call your friends. I"d rather have four quarters than one hundred pennies!

Steamo says never hate your enemy...it effects your judgement.

Steamo believes one of the important things to do before the morning comes is to let every one of your family and friends know that you care for them in simple ways and to let them know you love them, so they can always say, "He was my friend."

Steamo says lucky are those who find true, loyal friends in this fake world.

Steamo says you either love him or hate him. And if you love him, he's always in your heart. If you hate him, he's always on your mind. So either way, Steamo wins!

Steamo announced, "if you knew what was said in your absence, you'd stop smiling with a lot of people."

The quality of our enemies does us honor... or dishonor.

Steamo says not one scar on his heart came from his enemies. They all came from people who said they loved me.

Steamo has observed that social media has made us antisocial.

Steamo never regrets the love he puts out into the universe. Love always comes back full circle he says. Keep putting love into the universe - it"s coming back! It has to!

Steamo reminds us that nothing said before the word BUT really counts.

Steamo reminds us to be who we are! Those that mind, don't matter. And those that really matter, don't mind!

Steamo reminds us - Be careful who you help!

Steamo says to make a difference in someone's life, you don't have to be brilliant, rich, beautiful, or perfect. You just have to care.

Steamo says "Be kind to unkind people. They need it the most.

Steamo says stop serving good vibes to those that deserve GOODBYES!

Steamo reminds us that being too close to the wrong people can ruin you!

Chapter 5
Faith and Purpose

Sometimes life offers second chances, so never give up!

Steamo says one of the best lessons you can learn in life is to master how to remain calm. Being calm is a super power.

Steamo has learned that not all storms come to disrupt your life. Some come to clear your path.

Steamo says success is not always what you see.

Steamo advises those he mentors that a delay is not a denial.

Steamo believes the more you experience rejection, the more things you have to celebrate!

Steamo points out that for those who believe, no proof is necessary and for those that don't, no proof is possible.

Steamo reminds us that you never know how close you are...NEVER give up on your dreams!

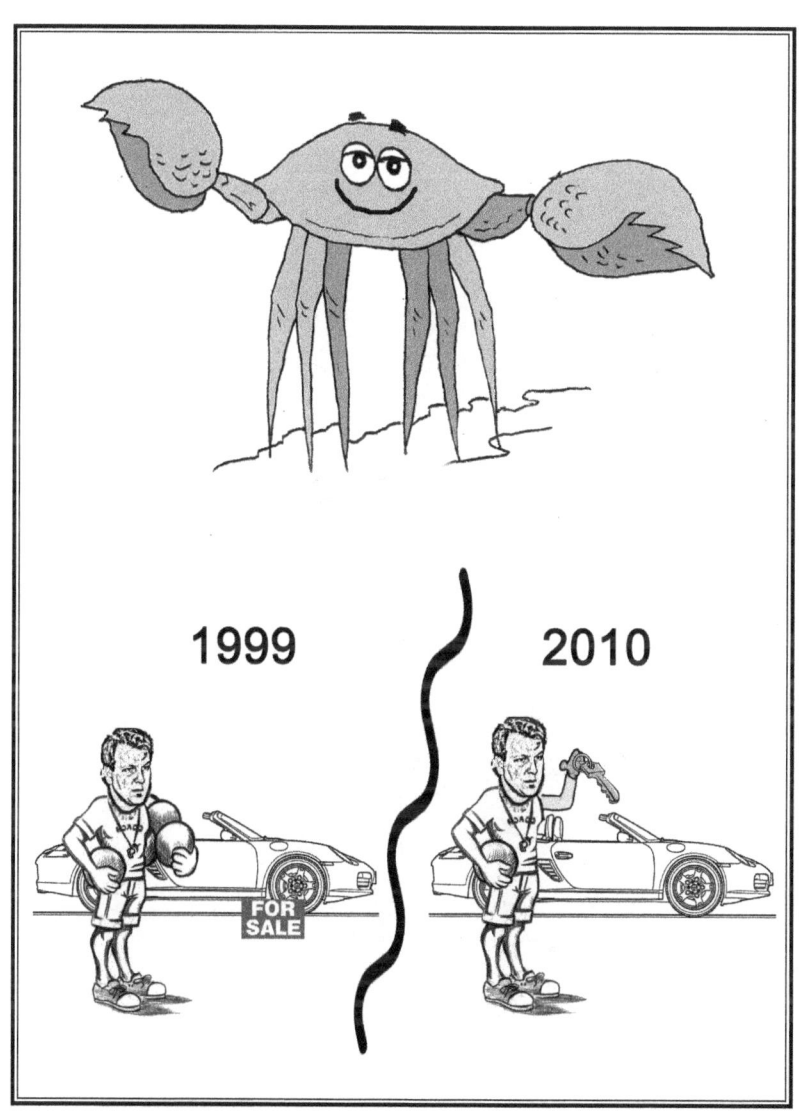

Lost dreams can be found again says Steamo!

Steamo believes that life is a gift. Use it to help other people use their gift.

Steamo reminds us - Things end. People leave. Time passes. Memories fade. Feelings change. And you know what? Life goes on.

Steamo reminds us if an egg is broken by outside force, life ends. If broken by inside force, life begins. Great things always begin from the inside.

When Steamo learned that Albert Einstein couldn't read until the 5th grade, he realized all things are possible when you have hope. Hope is the best of all things.

Steamo says "Television is a monster. And it's called a program for a reason - it's a mind altering device. It's designed to change the way you see reality."

Steamo says good deeds are not done by walking into a church. They are done when you walk out of the church and help others.

In a race between lion and deer, many times the deer wins because the lion runs for food and the deer runs for life. PURPOSE is more important than need.

Steamo says death is a reality most people can't consciously accept - and nobody knows a date, a time, or how.

Steamo advises that if you feel you are losing everything, remember that trees lose their leaves every year but they stand tall and wait for better days!

Steamo says Noah looked like he was an idiot until it started to rain. Keep building!

Steamo says the moment you start acting like life is a blessing, that's when it starts to feel like one!

Steamo reminds us that you ARE rich...when you are content and happy with what you have.

Chapter 6
Planning

Steamo says your dad can teach you a whole lot, including who you never want to be.

Steamo said to Mr. Anderson you don't have to be great to start, but you have to start to be great!

Steamo realizes that time is undefeated.

Steamo reminds us that when a flashlight grows dim, you don't throw it away. You change the batteries! So help someone change their batteries, or sit with them and share your light!

Steamo says there is no purpose in life. It is just happening. It's a matter of point of view.

To Steamo, direction is so much more important than speed. Many are going nowhere fast.

Steamo says you can only really control the controllables so don't worry about things you cannot control.

Steamo told Iraset Iraset that the veneer of civilization is pretty thin.

In Steamo's experience, the cheetah always knows where the hyena is.

Steamo told the coach "You have to keep the main thing the main thing!"

Chapter 7
Self and Growth

Steamo says "I care less about your potential and more about what you do with it. The world is full of gifted underachievers. Don't waste your gifts."

Steamo reminds us that conditioning is gradual but constant and destructive. All lead to "No I can't."

When Steamo is showing you the forest, stop staring at the tree!

Steamo wants to remind us that we don't know what we don't know.

Steamo heard that on average one person will influence 80,000 people in the course of their lifetime - enough to fill a football stadium!

After spending time with humans Steamo realized that most people spend their lives as if they have another one in the bank.

Once Steamo loses respect for you it's gone for good, he never re-respects someone.

Anyone can look at what they don't have, that's easy. Steamo says always be grateful and find a way to appreciate what you do have.

Steamo subscribes to the theory that "If wishes were horses, beggars would ride."

Steamo thinks we were born to win, and almost immediately we are conditioned to lose.

Steamo says that being kicked while you are down will turn you into a beast when you get back up.

Steamo says sometimes it is better to be wrong so someone else can be right.

Steamo said be grateful.

Chances of becoming a millionaire - 1%.
Chances of becoming a billionaire - .00002%.
Chances of winning the lottery - .000001%.
Chances of being born - .000000001%.
You had a 1 in a 400 TRILLION chance to be born!

You WON the day you took your first breath.

What are you doing with your winnings?

Steamo says closure is a myth. Don't fool yourself - it just doesn't happen.

Steamo says the time is here where people prefer to hear comforting lies than actually learning important but unpleasant truths.

Steamo told Soberanis, "If there is a choice between being average or being excellent, and if excellence is an option, how could you settle for being average?

Steamo said the past is behind us and the future is brighter than the past. "Dream again...dream big dreams!"

Steamo reminds us that you become what you feed your mind! Think positive!

Behavior can and often must be modified. Start by putting a smile on your face and act happy. Then make a conscious choice to be happy.

Steamo reminds us that gossip is not something to take part in.

Steamo reminds us that truth seems like hate to those who hate the truth.

Steamo reminds us to forget what hurt us. But never forget what it taught you!

Steamo said you can't push someone up the ladder unless they are willing to climb!

Steamo reminds us that when you're dead, you don't know you are dead. The pain is felt by others. The same is true if you are stupid.

Steamo advises to SPEAK in such a way that others will love to LISTEN to you. LISTEN in such a way that others love to SPEAK to you.

Chapter 8
Romance

Steamo told nurse Barb, "One day you'll find someone obsessed with you. It's probably going to be a dog. But it is what it is."

Steamo advises stop worrying about what others think and decide to be extraordinary.

Steamo learned that a woman's Who Who Ha Ha is undefeated!

Steamo observed that PUSSY is undefeated!

Steamo reminds us that your relationship doesn't need to make sense to anyone except you and your partner. It's not a community project.

Steamo reminds us that brilliance can't last forever. It's like a fireworks show - it ends.

Regarding dating: Steamo noticed the talent pool thins out as you age.

Steamo noticed if you call a woman beautiful 100 times she won't notice. But call her fat once and she will never forget.

Chapter 9
Common Sense

Steamo reminds us that food is the most abused anxiety drug. And exercise is the most underutilized antidepressant.

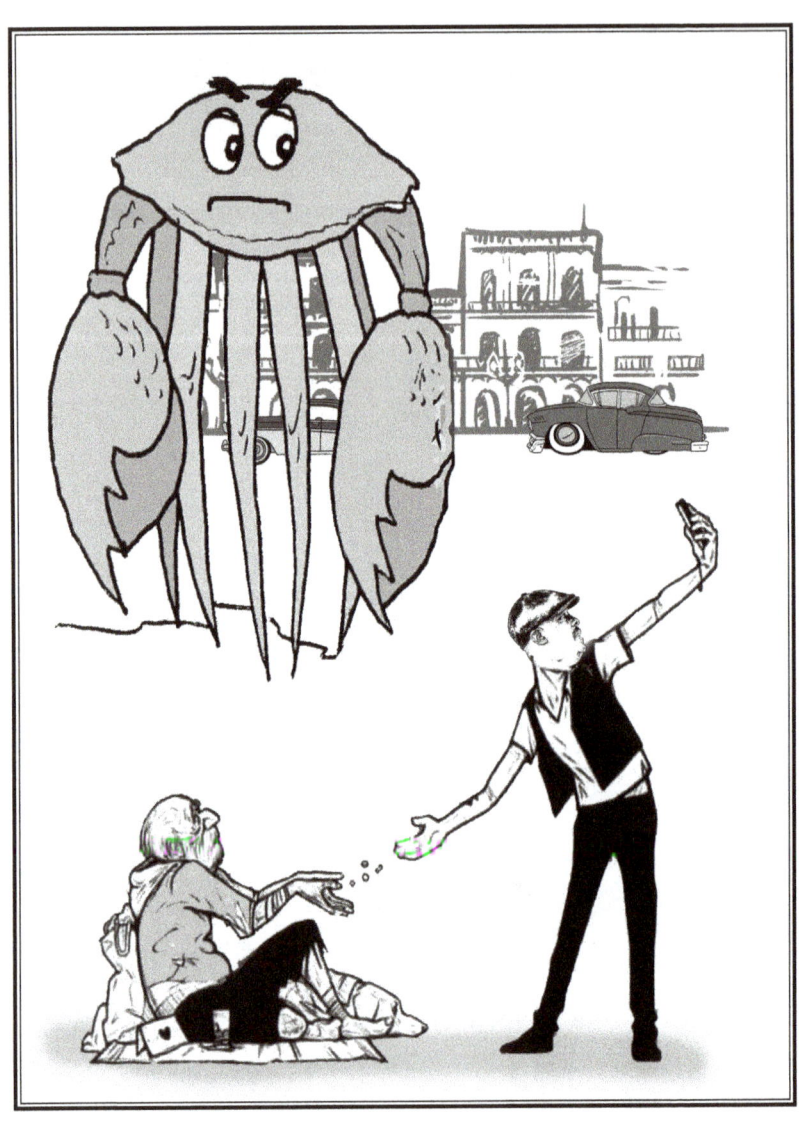

Steamo says a picture is worth a thousand words!

Steamo says you should always be yourself, unless you can be a pirate and then you should always be a pirate.

Steamo advises, when working for someone else, don't be complicated.

Steamo says common sense is not a gift. It's a punishment...because you have to deal with everyone who doesn't have it.

Steamo told the coach to watch out for people like this!

Steamo realizes one thing about getting older: Your eyesight starts getting weaker but your ability to see through people's bullshit gets much better.

Steamo reminds us that if someone has an emergency, and asks to borrow your car for 15 days, and they still have it 2 years later -- your car was stolen dude!

Steamo says. "I don't mean to brag, but I have the exact same medical degree as Bill Gates."

The Nobel Peace Prize was founded and named after the man who invented dynamite - incongruent thought Steamo.

Steamo never speaks wisdom into the ears of a fool because he will despise you for it.

Steamo told his friends it's hard to win an argument with a smart person, but it's damn near impossible to win an argument with a stupid person.

Coach Miller told Steamo, "Winners never quit!" Steamo: "Yes they do...they quit doing stupid shit."

Steamo says everything you say should be true, but not everything true should be said.

Steamo reminds us not to argue with stupid people. They bring you down to their level and then beat you with their experience.

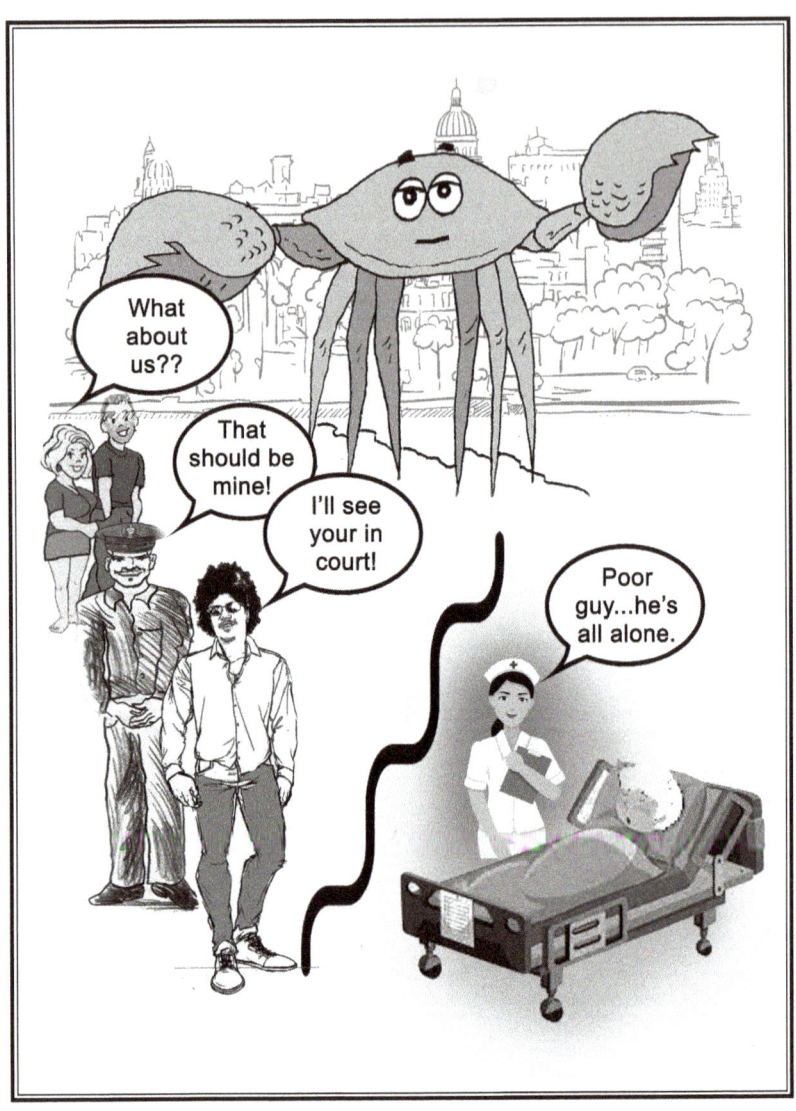

Steamo reminds us that people will fight over your money and anything you leave, but not over taking care of you when you're sick and dying.

Steamo says the best therapist has fur and four legs.

Steamo says if you want total security, go to prison. You'll be fed, clothed, and get medical care. But you'll have no FREEDOM!

Steamo reminds us that no one can destroy iron - except its own rust . Just like your own mind can destroy YOU!

Chapter 10
Anger and Punishment

Steamo says remember that the same people who did you wrong are telling a different version of the story...and they are playing the victim!

When asked what anger is, Steamo said it is the punishment we give ourselves for somebody else's mistake.

Steamo says two things define you: your patience when you have nothing and your attitude when you have everything.

Steamo reminds us that happy people make the world a better place.

Steamo says, "Oh, you hate me? Join the club! There are weekly meetings at the corner of Fuck You St. and Kiss My Ass Blvd.!"

Steamo thought - Why are people afraid of raccoons and police? For good reason, they are big and fierce and they bite hard!

Steamo noticed that people who can't communicate think everything is an argument.

Steamo says don't blame a clown for acting like a clown. Blame yourself for going to the circus.

Steamo said: "My silence doesn't mean I agree with you. It's just your stupidity has rendered me speechless."

If you ever want to know who people really are, watch and see how they treat people they THINK they don't need.

About the Author

Steamo goes to Havana is the creation of Dr. Michael Miller and his sixth published book. Most of his books, DVD's and numerous articles are focused on self-improvement.

Dr. Miller has traveled extensively in Cuba and previously wrote The Adventures of Steamo The Wonder Crab published in 2017.

Steamo goes to Havana is a continuation of the original book in a new setting and with some new characters.

Dr. Miller has been in education for over 35 years and has earned five college degrees, including three advanced degrees and is a modern day philosopher and acclaimed life coach.

Dr. Miller is a member of Masonic Lodge 327 located in Long Beach, California.

Minhee Choe is an animator, illustrator and author. She worked for DreamWorks Feature Animation, Warner Bros Feature Animation, Sony, ILM and other companies. She worked on Iron Giant, Shark Tale, Pirates of the Caribbean, Jurassic Park 3, Men in Black 2 and other feature films and commercials. She worked for Living Books on Dr. Suess titles, as well as other popular children's books. She is also an author and illustrator for Fun with Duckies. She resides in Los Angeles with her husband.

Jeffrey Vernon is a graphic designer and illustrator who has worked for advertising agencies and design studios throughout the eighties and nineties. He designed the packaging for Atari's Pac-Man, Ms. Pac-Man and others. Since 2020 he has worked as an independent contractor for authors, illustrating children's books and designing websites. Jeff illustrated the first Steamo book, "The Adventures of Steamo The Wonder Crab."

NEW FALCON PUBLICATIONS

2046 Hillhurst Avenue
Los Angeles, CA 90027

info@newfalcon.com
newfalcon.com